The Very Best
DOG

My Life Story as Told by My Human

WORKMAN PUBLISHING
NEW YORK

Library of Congress Cataloging-in-Publication Data
Names: Terhune, Becky, book designer.
Title: The very best dog : my life story as told by my human /
design by Becky Terhune ; illlustration by Youlie Dessine.
Description: New York : Workman Publishing, [2021]
Identifiers: LCCN 2021021136 | ISBN 9781523512324 (hardcover)
Subjects: LCSH: Dogs. | Dog owners.
Classification: LCC SF427 .V396 2021 | DDC 636.7/083--dc23
LC record available at https://lccn.loc.gov/2021021136

ISBN 978-1-5235-1232-4

Design by Becky Terhune
Illustration by Youlie Dessine

Workman books are available at special discounts when purchased in bulk for premiums and sales
promotions as well as for fundraising or educational use. Special editions or book excerpts can also be
created to specification. For details, contact the Special Sales Director at specialmarkets@workman.com.

Workman Publishing Co., Inc.
225 Varick Street
New York, NY 10014-4381

workman.com

WORKMAN is a registered trademark of Workman Publishing Co., Inc.

Printed in China
First printing February 2022

10 9 8 7 6 5 4 3 2 1

This book belongs to:

....
(write your name here)

More importantly, this book is about
the amazing, incomparable, one-of-a-kind,
best dog ever:

....

The First Time We Met

When we first met, it was ....
....
....

You were the dog who was ....
....
....
....

SNIFF SNIFF

And you were just so cute! I loved the way

your tail ....

and your ears..

....

And when you looked at me with your...

eyes, I knew we were meant for each other.

You were (check all that apply):

❑ eager, tiny, and irresistible

❑ a rambunctious teenager

❑ already grown-up, with just
the right energy level

❑ refined and mature

Paste a photo here.

Why I Chose You

The top three reasons I found you so irresistible:

1. ....

2. ....

3. ....

Your breed (or our best guess): ....

Your coat is (check all that apply):

❑ thick

❑ double-coated

❑ fluffy

❑ sleek and smooth

❑ wiry

❑ short

❑ shaggy

❑ long

❑ curly

❑ velvety

Your fur is (check all that apply):

❑ black

❑ brown

❑ red

❑ gray

❑ golden/yellow

❑ tan

❑ white

❑ spotted

❑ merle

❑ brindle

❑ sable

Your special details are (check all that apply):

❏ floppy ears
❏ stand-up ears
❏ folded ears
❏ smushed nose
❏ long nose
❏ flat face
❏ eye patch
❏ big eyes
❏ flappy jowls
❏ long tongue
❏ Other: ....
....
....
....

❏ neck wrinkles
❏ giant paws
❏ spindly legs
❏ stumpy legs
❏ fluffy tail
❏ curly tail
❏ whip tail
❏ otter tail
❏ nub or docked tail

I imagine our life together will be ....
....
....
....
....

When We Found Each Other

When I met you, you were living ....

I remember it being ....

At first, I thought you were .... because you were acting

.... After spending more

time with you, I realized you were really ....

Your most charming quality(-ies) is (are) ....

....

The first human I introduced you to was ....

When I brought you home, I was with ....

....

You wanted us to bring home certain toys, loveys, and other

mementos from where you'd been, so we brought

along ....

....

It was a big day! You were (check all that apply):

❑ nervous   ❑ quiet

❑ barking   ❑ wagging your tail

❑ excited   ❑ making a mess

❑ calm   ❑ Other: ....

❑ growling   ....

❑ antsy   ....

One memorable thing you did on the way home was ....

....

....

Paste some photos here of your dog's life
before you brought him/her home.

What's in a Name?

List of names I considered:

....

....

....

....

....

....

....

....

....

....

Your name before we met was ....

The name I chose is ....

I chose it because ....

....

I often call you nicknames like ....

....

....

....

My weirdest nickname for you is ....

It was an obvious choice because ....

....

....

Top five songs that I sing with your name woven into the lyrics:

1. ....

2. ....

3. ....

4. ....

5. ....

Paste some photos here of your dog's first family or of the people who cared for him/her before you met.

Your Family, Then and Now

We ❏ did ❏ did not get to meet your mom or dad.

Your parents were:

❏ of .... breed

❏ of an unknown breed

You had:

❏ .... siblings

❏ brothers from another mother

❏ sisters from another mister

We may not know a lot about your parents, but we learned about your ancestry! Here are your DNA test results:

.... % .... % ....

.... % .... % ....

.... % .... % ....

.... % .... % ....

.... % .... % ....

Now that you've joined the family, you have .... siblings!

They are:

Name: ....

Species/breed: ....

How you are similar (or different):

....

....

....

Name: ....

Species/breed: ....

How you are similar (or different):

....

....

....

Name: ....

Species/breed: ....

How you are similar (or different):

....

....

....

Name: ....

Species/breed: ....

How you are similar (or different):

....

....

....

Paste some photos of your dog's family—then and now—here.

Welcome Home!

This is where we live!

Paste a photo here.

I made you a cozy corner to help you settle in.

Here's what's in it:

....

....

....

The first toy I bought you was

....

Your First Day

We are so glad you're here!

The first thing you did at home was

....

....

....

....

....

The Story of Your Homecoming

....

....

....

....

....

....

....

....

....

....

....

....

....

....

....

....

Your Beauty Regimen

You are groomed:

❑ by me

❑ at the groomer's

❑ You don't need grooming!

You get baths:

❑ almost every day

❑ weekly

❑ monthly

❑ once in a blue moon

❑ only when sprayed by a skunk

How you feel about bath time (check all that apply):

❑ splish-splash!

❑ indifferent

❑ reluctant

❑ bribery required

❑ terrified

❑ the ultimate betrayal

Paste some photos of your dog in his/her most fetching getup.

Your Sleep Routine

On average, you sleep .... hours a day.

Your favorite spot for a snooze is ....
....
....
....
....
....

Enjoy your nap!

Paste a photo of your dog enjoying
a nap in his/her favorite spot here.

Your Personality

On the first few days, you were:

☐ calm   ☐ grumpy

☐ playful   ☐ sassy

☐ fearful   ☐ silly

☐ bossy   ☐ still adjusting

After a few weeks, you were

....

....

....

....

Now, you are

....

....

....

....

If you were a crystal or a precious stone, you would be

....

If you were a plant, you would be ....

If you were a song, you would be ....

If you were a celebrity, you would be ....

If you were a character from a movie, you would be

....

Happy Tails

Paste a photo of your contented pup here.

Here's what you do to get my attention:

You whine to tell me ....

Sometimes you growl at ....

You wag your tail when ....

You get very excited when it's time for ....

....

....

....

At mealtimes, you ....

....

....

At the Vet

Your first vet visit was

....

....

Our First Trip to the Vet: A Story

....

....

....

....

....

....

....

....

Paste a photo here.

After One Month...

Our morning routine was ....

....

....

....

We had to take you outside every .... ❏ minutes ❏ hours.

Our usual walking route was ....

....

You preferred to sleep ....

....

You had grown:

❏ a little

❏ like a weed

❏ up

I first noticed you coming out of your shell when ....

....

....

....

Your personality was ....

....

....

....

You acquired the new nicknames ....

....

....

....

Paste a photo here.

Our Home

Your favorite places are

....

....

....

You never go

....

....

....

....

Your secret hiding spot is

....

....

....

....

What you do to tell me you need to go out:

....

....

....

Paste some photos here.

Playtime

You mostly play:

- ❑ with chew toys
- ❑ with balls
- ❑ with flying discs
- ❑ with rope toys
- ❑ with stuffed animals
- ❑ with other dogs
- ❑ with cats
- ❑ with humans

- ❑ with me
- ❑ by yourself
- ❑ at the dog park
- ❑ You don't play much.
- ❑ You don't care much for toys, all you want is TREATS!
- ❑ Other: ....
  ....

When I'm not watching, you like to play with ....
....

The funniest toy you've invented is ....
....

The funniest thing you do while playing is ....
....

Your wrestling style is ....
....

Capturing Your Silly Side

Paste some funny photos of your pup here.

Paste some photos here of your dog playing.

Best Buds for Six Months!

Paste a photo here.

Paste some photos here.

Wag Therapy

You always brighten my day.

Some of my favorite mood-lifting moments:

....

....

....

....

....

....

....

Our First Adopt-iversary!

What we did to celebrate:

....

....

....

....

....

....

Paste a photo here.

Paste some photos here.

Your Style

Your collar is ....

Your harness is ....

Your funniest accessories are ....

....

....

....

Your cleverest costumes are ....

....

....

....

Your thoughts about wearing clothes are ....

....

....

....

Paste some photos here.

Your Eating Habits

For meals, we give you ....,
and you eat .... times throughout
the day.

You eat:
❑ a little bit
❑ just enough
❑ a lot
❑ too much

You love:

....

....

....

....

....

....

....

....

You hate:

....

....

....

....

....

....

When I got you, you weighed ....

Paste a photo here.

After a year, you weighed ....

Paste a photo here.

Our Wanderings and Explorations

On the weekends, I sometimes take you to ....

If we stay home, we ....

....

You love (check all that apply):

❏ running in the grass

❏ rolling in the grass

❏ getting zoomies

❏ splashing in the rain

❏ sniffing flowers

❏ eating mushrooms

❏ eating poop

❏ chasing birds and squirrels

❏ wrestling

❏ frolicking in the snow

❏ visiting the dog park

❏ getting puppaccinos on
   coffee dates

❏ hiking on trails

❏ climbing mountains

❏ performing neighborhood
   watch duties

❏ being my copilot

❏ Other: ....

Parks we've been to: ....

....

....

....

....

....

....

Paste a photo here.

Your First Training Session

The first trick you learned was ....

....

The skills you learned quickly were ....

....

The tricks you're still working on are ....

....

Games you love (check all that apply):

❑ scavenger hunts for treats

❑ hide-and-seek

❑ catching a ball or Frisbee

❑ tug-of-war

❑ which hand has the treat?

❑ puzzle toys

❑ "hot and cold"

❑ Other: ....

Paste a photo here.

Our First Holiday

I gave you

....

....

....

....

....

Your favorite treat was ....

....

....

....

You got into mischief with ....

....

....

....

You loved playing with the ....

We spent the holidays ....

....

Paste a photo here.

Our Secret Language

When you want .... ,
you ....
....
....
....

When you nose or paw me,
you're telling me that

....
....
....
....

....

You sometimes whine to tell me that ....

You growl to indicate ....

You vocalize (check all that apply):

❑ most of the time   ❑ when you're hungry

❑ rarely   ❑ when you're happy

❑ when I get home   ❑ when you want snuggles

❑ in the middle of the night   ❑ Other: ....

❑ in the morning   ....

Your happy sounds are ....

....

You are most talkative when ....

....

I know that you're getting mad when ....

....

Sometimes You're Naughty . . .

Your worst offense:

....

....

....

....

....

Your funniest offense:

....

....

....

....

Your messiest offense:

....

....

....

....

....

Your first offense:

....

....

....

....

....

....

Paste a mugshot here.

Our First Big Adventure

The first time we traveled, it was to

....

....

....

....

....

....

We traveled by:

❏ boat

❏ car

❏ plane

❏ train

You've already visited:

....

....

....

....

....

....

....

....

....

....

....

....

....

....

....

Your Pawprints

Press your dog's paw onto a pet-safe ink pad. Next, press the paw to the paper, within the yellow shape below. Be sure to apply pressure evenly to get a complete print. To avoid smudging, try to keep the paw still while it's pressed to the page. Slowly lift the paw from the page and immediately wash your dog's paw.

We've Been Living Together for Two Years!

Paste some photos here.

Your Schedule

A TYPICAL DAY	
8 a.m.–10 a.m.	
10 a.m.–12 p.m.	
12 p.m.–2 p.m.	
2 p.m.–6 p.m.	
6 p.m.–8 p.m.	
8 p.m.–10 p.m.	
10 p.m.–12 a.m.	
12 a.m.–8 a.m.	

Your Daily Activities

Your favorite exercise/
activities are ....
....
....
....

Every day, you play with
....
....
....
....
....
....
....

Your Turf

Who do you let into the house? ....

....

When the doorbell rings, you ....

....

Do you enjoy having human guests? ....

What about other doggy guests? ....

Do you have a relationship with the mail carrier
or package delivery person? ....

When I leave the house, you ....

....

....

When we see other dogs on walks, you ....

....

....

Your other habits on walks (check all that apply):

- ❑ You like to mark things.
- ❑ You think that everything must be sniffed.
- ❑ You're a dilly-dallyer.
- ❑ You're eager to be out in front.
- ❑ You stay right by my side.
- ❑ You tend to drag behind.
- ❑ You believe that all wildlife must be chased.
- ❑ You love to meet ....
  ....
- ❑ You display a total indifference toward other creatures.
- ❑ Other: ....

You love to spend time:

- ❑ in the yard
- ❑ on the balcony
- ❑ in the park
- ❑ Other: ....

Are you jealous?

- ❑ Yes
- ❑ No

Of who? ....

....

Part of the Family

Your connection with other family
members is ....
....
....

You love

....

....

....

You don't like

....

....

....

....

You're not interested in

....

....

....

....

Paste some photos here of your
dog with members of your family.

Your Animal Friends

You befriended

....

....

....

....

You share your life with

....

....

....

You don't like

.... very much.

Paste some photos here of
your dog with other animals.

Snuggles and Scratches

You love when I pet your ....

This is how you ask to be petted: ....

When I want to tease you, I just have to scratch your ....

....

Your thoughts on ear rubs are ....

You request belly rubs when ....

Where you prefer to be scratched: ....

Paste a photo here.

SCRATCH
SCRATCH

Your Favorite Furniture

Paste a photo here.

Your favorite piece of furniture to nap on is ....

Your favorite blanket is ....

You ❑ are ❑ are not allowed on the bed . . . and this is how
you feel about it: ....

....

Paste some photos here.

We've Already Been Together for Three Years!

Paste a photo here.

Paste some photos here.

You Love . . .

Your favorite TV show is ....

Your favorite people food is ....

Your favorite toy is ....

Your favorite song is ....

Your favorite spot to sniff is ....

Your favorite dog park is ....

Your best friend is ....

Top five things you love to eat:

1. ....

2. ....

3. ....

4. ....

5. ....

Paste a photo here.

You Hate . . .

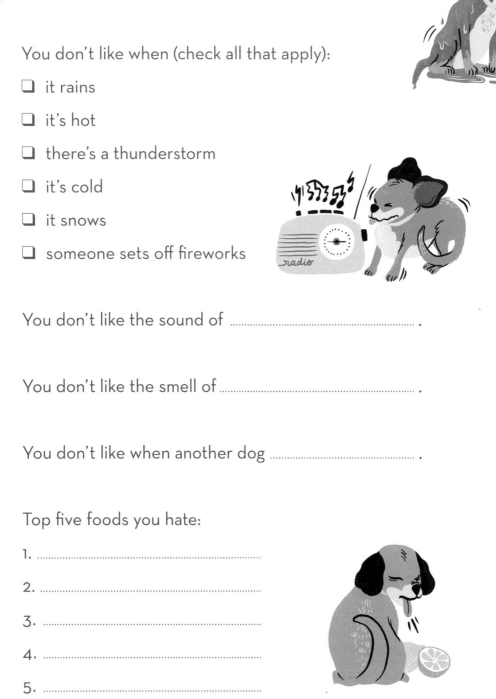

You don't like when (check all that apply):

❑ it rains

❑ it's hot

❑ there's a thunderstorm

❑ it's cold

❑ it snows

❑ someone sets off fireworks

You don't like the sound of ....

You don't like the smell of ....

You don't like when another dog ....

Top five foods you hate:

1. ....

2. ....

3. ....

4. ....

5. ....

Our Best Memories

Paste some photos here.

Our Most Adorable Selfies

Paste some photos here.

Paste some photos here.

On Vacation

I've left you in the care of

....

....

while

....

....

You were:

❑ happy

❑ sad

❑ indifferent

You love when

....

....

takes care of you.

Your Report Card

Playtime:

- ❑ active
- ❑ cuddly
- ❑ excited
- ❑ talkative
- ❑ shy
- ❑ friendly
- ❑ grumpy
- ❑ antisocial
- ❑ low energy

Meals:

- ❑ hungry
- ❑ thirsty
- ❑ steady eater
- ❑ slow to partake
- ❑ selective

Behaviors:

- ❑ happy
- ❑ playful
- ❑ anxious
- ❑ quiet
- ❑ boisterous
- ❑ energetic
- ❑ sleepy

Paste some photos here.

Sitting Pretty

Paste some photos here.

Paste some photos here.

Portrait of an Adventurer

Paste some photos here.

Paste some photos here.